DECORATING WITH

WREATHS, GARLANDS, TOPIARIES

AND BOUQUETS

DECORATING WITH
WREATHS, GARLANDS, TOPIARIES
AND BOUQUETS

CAROL ENDLER STERBENZ

Photography by
Steven Mays

Styling by
Sylvia Lachter

RIZZOLI
NEW YORK

ACKNOWLEDGMENTS

I am grateful to the many friends and colleagues who so generously supported this project and whose special talents helped make this book possible. I would like to thank especially: Steven Mays, the photographer, who captured and enhanced on film what was in my imagination, and his assistant, Robert Whitcomb; Sylvia Lachter, stylist, who beautifully assembled all the components into an aesthetic whole, and whose contribution was far greater (as usual) than can be described; Lois Brown, of Rizzoli, who believed in me all along the way and was a compelling force in bringing this work to publication; and Christina Bliss, who designed *Decorating with Wreaths, Garlands, Topiaries and Bouquets* with skill and sensitivity.

I would also like to express my heartfelt thanks to the many friends whose generous hospitality permitted us to photograph the designs in exceptional interiors and pastoral surroundings: Jo and Ralph Alfenito, Diane and Robert Kirchner, Mary Ann and Christopher Pettit, Janet and Charles Vaccaro, and Bonnie and John Williamson. And thank you to those whose doors were opened wide in spirit: Sharon and Candy Fuentes, Jean and Kent Gale, Nancy and James Johnson, Woodie and David Sims, and Heather and Tom Tucker, as well as Andy Schmitz of Andrew Schmitz III & Associates.

A very special thanks to Judy Duhaime for preparing the spring desserts, to Virginia Gray and to Guy Reuge of Restaurant Mirabelle in St. James, New York, for the autumn desserts.

I am also grateful to the local Huntington, New York, businesses and store owners who so enthusiastically loaned their products: Sandy Chapin and Mary Ann Pettit of Adobe Artes; Sue Pitiger of Three Sisters and Janet Vaccaro of Willow Pond Antiques, two extraordinary shops within Baycrest Antiques and Designs; Jackie Ambriano, Vivien Forgione, Carol Buck, and Jane Sloan of Chartier; Michael N. Minella of Culinary Studio; Fern Folz of Fern's Creative Thimble; Dave and Adolph Aebisher of Fort Hill Nurseries and Florist; Jonathan Randall of Jonathan's; Sarah Coulson-Latham and Janice Hubers of Scentsational; and Bonnie Waterman and Ted Ryder of Seaholm Wines and Liquors. And a sincere thanks to Vaban Ribbons International for the exquisite ribbons and to Wilton Armatelle for the pewter.

This project could never have been accomplished, no less contemplated, without the inspirational "presence" of Sheila Heller and the love and encouragement of my husband, John, and children, Genevieve, Rodney, and Gabrielle. Many kisses.

Library of Congress Cataloging-in-Publication Data

Sterbenz, Carol Endler.
Decorating with wreaths, garlands, topiaries, and bouquets / Carol Endler Sterbenz ;
photography by Steven Mays ; styling by Sylvia Lachter.
p.   cm.
Includes bibliographical references (p.) and index.
ISBN 0-8478-1651-6
1. Wreaths.   2. Flower arrangement in interior decoration.
3.Topiary work.   I. Title.
SB449.5.W74S74 1993
745.92—dc20   92-42981
CIP

Editor: Lois Brown
Design by Christina Bliss

Printed in Singapore

IMPORTANT NOTE TO THE READER: Every effort has been made to present the information in this book in a clear, complete, and accurate manner. It is important that all instructions be carefully followed as failure to do so could result in injury, and the Publisher and Author expressly disclaim any and all liability resulting therefrom.

TABLE OF CONTENTS

INTRODUCTION

*D*ECORATING WITH WREATHS, GARLANDS, TOPIARIES, AND BOUQUETS *is foremost a decorating and style book that reveals the vast possibilities the floral arts afford us as "home furnishings"—whether used as a simple accent or as an eye-catching centerpiece. Each page of this lavishly illustrated book will lead you on a walk through fine home interiors and exteriors that have been enhanced by specially designed floral arrangements for every season of the year. The majority are made of dried flowers and foliage, but several feature silk components for practicality's sake. The text offers an abundance of unique decorating and gift ideas to inspire you, followed by encouraging step-by-step directions to help you create each design featured.*

And that is one of the particularly appealing aspects of DECORATING WITH WREATHS, GARLANDS, TOPIARIES, AND BOUQUETS: All of the designs in the collection can be made by following only four basic construction techniques and using readily available materials, no matter what your level of craft experience. A handy Source Directory provides a nationwide guide to retail stores, crafts shops, garden centers, mail-order companies and manufacturers that supply high-quality dried flowers, foliage, and supplies as well as ready-made arrangements.

Though we may traditionally associate wreaths and the like with Christmas (and there is an entire section devoted to this enchanting time), this book reinterprets these decorations for year-long display. Spring flowers burst forth in designs that fill cold hearths, arch above windows and doors, and drape shelves and chairs. Summer designs in buttercup yellow and poppy red enhance outdoor entertaining, and live flowers adorn a maypole topiary. Rich earth colors like burnt orange and copper find expression in autumn arrangements—wheat bouquets, lush floral cascades, and untamed garlands of silver birch and bittersweet.

What you will quickly discover is that wreaths, garlands, topiaries, and bouquets are the perfect answer for enhancing any space. No occasion need be excluded, no room neglected, no nook or cranny left out. A boa of herbs that dressed up an old wagon for a party gets draped over a kitchen beam and provides a flavorsome addition to the evening meal; after a festive feast, a tiny butterfly-shaped napkin ring rests on a bedside table in the guest room. When you see a wall that needs "something," you will begin to consider the versatile wreath; or perhaps you will find an irresistible garland and rearrange a room to accommodate it.

DECORATING WITH WREATHS, GARLANDS, TOPIARIES, AND BOUQUETS captures all the beauty and appeal of the floral crafts and is certain to beguile even the most reluctant home decorator. You may even find yourself saving fallen pinecones, scrutinizing roadway shoulders, and rescuing discarded bits of ribbon. If the fragrance of one branch of balsam causes you to imagine a forest of Christmas trees or if you begin to daydream about spring bouquets of tea roses while the back steps are wrapped in snow, then this treasury is meant for you.

BASIC CONSTRUCTION MATERIALS

*T*HE WORK CUPBOARD. *The open doors of this antique pine cupboard reveal an array*

of dried flowers, ornamental grasses, and rolls and rolls of ribbon, along with the tools and supplies

that are commonly used to make any wreath, garland, topiary, or bouquet. Stacks of dried materials

are piled on top of the cupboard, and a finished hydrangea wreath hangs on the inside of the door

on the right.

The beauty of working with dried and silk flowers is that with only a few basic materials and tools, plus the knowledge of four basic construction techniques, you will be able to make any wreath, garland, topiary, or bouquet shown in this collection. With a little practice, you will soon be able to design your own decorations to fit your personal needs and taste.

THE WORK TABLE

TOPIARY	GARLAND	WREATH
PREPARED BASE	PREPARED FLOWERS	MOSS-COVERED WREATH
FLOWER POT	BOUQUETS	MATCHING THREAD
PLASTER OF PARIS	WIRE BASE	WIRE STAPLES
TRUNK	FINISHED GARLAND	SHEET MOSS
SHEET MOSS	WIRE ON REEL	HYDRANGEA
BOXWOOD SPRIGS	FLORAL TAPE	PARTIALLY DECORATED WREATH
DRY-FOAM HEAD	SHARP SCISSORS	
FINISHED TOPIARY		

Decorating with Wreaths, Garlands, and Topiaries

BASIC MATERIALS AND TOOLS

The following is a list of the materials and tools used to create the designs in this collection.

MATERIALS:
Frames: ready-made or as desired
Dried and silk flowers, foliage, and plant material
Stub wires: fine-gauge in varying lengths from 6"–11" (15cm–28cm)
    medium-gauge (wrapped) in 15½" length (40 cm)
    medium-gauge (painted) in 6" length (15 cm)
Wire on reel: fine-gauge
    medium-gauge
Waxed string on reel
Floral tape
Floral picks
Narrow adhesive tape
Plaster of paris
Floral clay
Floral spikes

TOOLS:
Sharp knife
Florist's scissors
Wire cutters
Pruning shears
Hot-glue gun and glue sticks*

*IMPORTANT: A HOT-GLUE GUN SHOULD BE USED WITH CAUTION, SINCE IT DISPENSES A SUPERHEATED STREAM OF LIQUID GLUE THAT CAN BURN YOU. ALWAYS UNPLUG THE GUN WHEN IT'S NOT IN USE. KEEP A BOWL OF ICE WATER NEARBY FOR ACCIDENTAL BURNS. KEEP CHILDREN AWAY FROM THE GUN.

*T*he frost lies soft—and
        thick—and white
Upon the fields and in the air...
On poplar trees—as if in prayer
And Orchard—mystical—apart—
The unborn Spring within her heart...

—M.E. Mason

THE DESIGNS OF WINTER

Winter

It is natural that we harmonize our spirits with the changing palette of the season, and winter brings a seemingly narrow set of choices that might at first appear skeletal and stark. But upon closer inspection, it is clear that the lack of color has been made up for in texture and clarity of line. Evergreen trees present a vast variety of color and texture, from pine and balsam to fir and spruce. When combined together and accented with other naturals, such as lady apples, pinecones, and berries, these winter offerings become beautiful and sophisticated designs to cheer up doors, tables, walls, and stairways.

The branches of trees and bushes also provide inspiration for distinctive arrangements. An armload of slender branches bound into a bundle becomes a sophisticated, contemporary accent for a den or living room; medallions of dried flowers of any kind and color can add a bit of romance.

And the excitement of Christmas provides an occasion for weeks and weeks of preparation as well as weeks and weeks to enjoy our work—from miniature creations that enhance gift packages, table settings, and sentimental objects like candlesticks and clock finials to more majestic statements as sumptuous garlands of fresh greenery draped over doorways, tables, and chairs. There is simply nothing like the scent of pine and balsam, and we can unleash our enthusiasm as we create a fragrant dwelling place for our family and friends, and our spirits.

HOLIDAY DOOR WREATH. A traditional evergreen wreath appears sophisticatedly untamed when made with three different kinds of evergreen boughs and decorated with red roses, everlastings, berries, and clusters of white bruneia sprigs. Encircled with a wire-edged metallic ribbon of deep strawberry, an otherwise traditional wreath evokes the pleasure of coming in from the cold to the warmth of a fireplace. This same wreath could be displayed inside using bunches of fresh white roses tied into clusters with gold mesh ribbon, allowing the long streamers to cascade in crinkly shapes.

*H*OLIDAY FOYER ENSEMBLE:

❧ *GARLAND FOR CLOCK — A delicate garland of balsam, with twigs sprayed copper, is accented with deep-red everlastings, roses, and berries and finished with an antique ribbon embroidered with metallic cord and weighted with gold balls.*

❧ *WREATH — Made by combining a rectangular frame of birch with a half circle of vine, this unconventional combination is then covered with sheet moss and decorated with flowers and pods in red and gold.*

❧ *TOPIARY — Faded green boxwood carpets the head of this topiary set in a faux concrete urn and created by Village Flowers of Huntington, New York. The boughs are decorated for the holiday with shiny red berries and gold balls, and the trunk is made from several lengths of grapevine and wrapped in a ribbon. Pinecones sprayed gold and dark-red everlastings accent a base covered in sphagnum moss.*

*C*HRISTMAS ENSEMBLE: ❧ MANTEL GARLAND — *The subtle Victorian colors of dusty rose, faded teal blue and white suggest an era of cut-crystal powder boxes and engraved silver. This romantic garland is made with bouquets of roses, hydrangeas, and pods; because the material is heavy, a base is fashioned from a dowel extended with wire tails so that a relatively rigid, weight-bearing center appears softer. Wire loops are attached for hanging.*

❧ *SPIRAL GARLAND — A spiral of velvety cockscomb, roses, and berries is actually a garland, with the size and fullness determined by a wired raffia base that is twisted, then decorated by hot-gluing bunches of floral material.*

❧ *CHRISTMAS TREE GARLAND — Small bunches of roses, hydrangeas, and leaves sprayed gold are used to create this flexible but fragile garland for the tree. The base of medium-gauge wire is wound with floral tape to provide a nonslip surface. Since the wire will twist somewhat as you bind on the bouquets, it is wise to leave some space between each one to prevent the dried materials from breaking.*

21

FATHER CHRISTMAS SHELF ENSEMBLE: ❧ *SPIRAL GARLAND — The fullness of this garland is one of its appeals, along with the strong contrast between red, magenta, and cream. It also makes a beautiful and unique wreath when made from a longer base. This garland is particularly time-consuming to make because most of the material is hot-glued in place.* ❧ *GOLD LEAF SWAG — Deriving its name from the drape of the leaves, this delicate garland is made simply by threading leaves sprayed gold on a length of thread; it is easy to make, with a vast choice of suitable materials. Try threading dried fruit for a country look, or rosebuds for something more romantic.* ❧ *TWIG BUNDLES — Humble twig bundles are transformed into elegant simplicity with a spray of metallic paint in copper. Choosing only the most slender, multibranched twigs of birch and binding them into little bundles takes very little time, but the effect is exquisite. You will enjoy making several dozen to leave all through the house, perhaps placed casually on a shelf or gathered in clusters and nestled in the bough of an evergreen wreath.*

CAUTION: EXTREME CARE MUST BE TAKEN WHEN PLACING DRIED MATERIALS NEAR CANDLES OR FLAME OF ANY KIND. TO AVOID CREATING A FIRE HAZARD, NEVER PLACE A DECORATION NEXT TO A FLAME; IF LIT CANDLES ARE USED, KEEP THEM A SAFE DISTANCE FROM THE DECORATION AND STAY IN THE ROOM TO KEEP A VIGILANT EYE.

Decorating with Wreaths, Garlands, and Topiaries

*C*HRISTMAS TABLE SETTING. *This country-style dining room features a long, antique pine table set for Christmas supper; red- and-green-checked rims of white dinner plates gleam against pewter chargers and the red goblets:* ❧ NATURAL CENTERPIECE—*An antique hand-hewn wooden bowl holds an array of pinecones and acorns sprayed gold, pods, cinnamon sticks, and rusty-red pomegranates. Holiday sparkle is added by the scattering of tiny gold balls and sprayed leaves, and a drizzle of red satin ribbon scribbles on top and creates a cozy warmth.* ❧ TABLE GARLANDS—*Lush evergreen boas crisscross at the table's center, and little bears tumble through greenery decorated with clusters of white bruneia sprigs, gold acorns, and shiny red berries. These garlands could easily be "faked" by laying the evergreen boughs directly on the table.* ❧ NATURALS IN MINIATURE FLOWER POTS—*Fill little terracotta flower pots to overflowing with miniature pinecones and shiny decorations; hide a small charm in one and give the finder a special gift.* ❧ MINIATURE TWIG TREES—*Rustic, spiky Christmas trees look great in this country setting; they're made by binding small bouquets of twigs together along a central trunk made from wire covered in brown floral tape, a construction similar to the garland's.*

*C*ANDLESTICK TOPIARIES. *The bases of these elegant topiaries are actually matching pewter candlesticks! Insert the stems of tea roses and white mallee eucalyptus leaves directly into the dry-foam (held in place by adhesive tape) until the entire head is lushly covered.*

Decorating with Wreaths, Garlands, and Topiaries

*T*ABLE ACCENTS: ❧ *TUSSIE-MUSSIE* — *A simple bouquet of roses, lavender, and silver artemisia is tied with a deep-teal French wired ribbon. Once popular for protecting the nose from street odors and believed to guard the body from the plague (when herbs with medicinal powers were used), today tussie-mussies are the perfect gift for a hostess or drop-in guests. Other bouquet combinations could include stems of statice, delphinium, larkspur, and cornflowers. For a romantic tussie-mussie, wrap the stems of the bouquet in antique lace.*

$\mathcal{V}$ASE BOUQUET. *Stems of mop-headed hydrangeas in blue and peach billow in mounds above this cut-crystal vase. Available in abundance in late summer and early autumn, hydrangeas dry standing in an inch or two of water and last throughout the long winter months. After you have enjoyed the vase of hydrangeas, consider making a wall garland from the dried flowers. Bind the stems of the hydrangeas into a long, stiff boa about two feet long; make a second boa and connect them together to form one long garland. Hot-glue deep pink roses, or orange bittersweet, to decorate the garland, and hang the garland over a doorway or a window.*

$\mathcal{B}$EDROOM ENSEMBLE:
❧ HEADBOARD
GARLAND—*This sumptuous
Gainsborough garland is made
from silk hydrangeas in dark
cranberry, light pink, and cream
combined with silk roses in white
and cream. Black berries and a
profusion of rose leaves frame the
expanse, along with a French
wired ribbon in avocado and
pink.* ❧ *NIGHT TABLE
TOPIARY— A stand of roses,
yellow everlastings, and
ranunculus is placed in a forties-
style ceramic flowerpot in
buttercup yellow. Stands of any
dried flowers with stiff stems can
be inserted in any configuration
into a block of dry-foam; be
careful to place the flower stems
in straight lines if a formal
pattern is desired.*

Decorating with Wreaths, Garlands, and Topiaries

*C*ORNER ACCENT: ❧ BASKET OF LAVENDER—*Referred to as a standard, this arrangement of lavender stems resembles a fan-shaped dome; placed in a birch basket and decorated with a wired ribbon threaded in front and behind the stems at the basket's perimeter, this design was created by Village Flowers. Its compact handsomeness is ideal for a corner shelf or small table.*

*B*ATHROOM ENSEMBLE: ❧ WALL GARLANDS—*Made to resemble a placard, each garland in this matching pair is made from a base of braided raffia. Bouquets of love-lies-bleeding, rose veronica, top brush, rough thistle grass, protea flat, and nigella are secured separately, working from the ends toward the center; larger pods and dried materials are glued in a central medallion shape.* ❧ SHELF GARLAND—*Due to the diminutive size and fragility of this garland, only three basic types of materials have been used. The components are held together by binding each tiny bouquet with sewing thread in a coordinating color.*

MATERIALS FOR WINTER COLLECTION

This chart offers an overview of this collection by listing the dried materials, the decorative form (wreath, garland, topiary, or bouquet), and the predominant color scheme for each of the designs featured.

WINTER DESIGNS	PG.	FORM	MATERIALS	COLOR SCHEME
Holiday Door Wreath	16	Wreath	Evergreen boughs; red foliage; red hybrid tea roses; dark red everlastings; red berries; white bruneia sprigs; leaves sprayed gold; strawberry colored metallic ribbon; metallic red poinsettias; gold balls.	Red/White/Green
HOLIDAY FOYER ENSEMBLE: Garland for Clock	18–19	Garland	Evergreen boughs; rose leaves; red hybrid tea roses; dark red everlastings; twigs sprayed copper; berries: red and gold; gold balls; ribbon; antique gold; tassels on cord	Red/Gold/Green
Square Wreath With Arched Top	18–19	Wreath	Sheet moss; red hybrid berries: red and gold; dark red everlastings; rose leaves; acorns; pods; seeds; gold balls; ribbon: gold and plaid; cord: gold and red; gold bell.	Red/Gold/Green
Conical Topiary	18–19	Topiary	Boxwood sprigs: grapevine; sphagnum moss; pinecones sprayed gold; red everlastings; red berries; gold balls; ribbon.	Green
CHRISTMAS ENSEMBLE: Garland for Mantel	20	Garland	Mop-headed hydrangeas: purple-tinged, lime green, blue; hybrid tea roses: pink, cerise-tinged, pale yellow; leucophylla; poppy seed heads; red berries; pods; leaves and pine cones sprayed gold.	Pink/Blue/Gold
Spiral Garland For Fireplace	20	Garland	Cockscomb:cream, deep red, deep magenta, pink; hybrid tea roses: red, pink, cream; white mallee eucalyptus leaves and miniature pinecones sprayed gold; red berries.	Red/Cream
Christmas Tree Garland	20	Garland	Mop-headed hydrangea florets: pink, blue,cream; hybrid tea roses: pink, cream, pale yellow; white ranunculus; leaves and pinecones sprayed gold.	Pink/Blue

Decorating With Wreaths, Garlands, and Topiaries

WINTER DESIGNS	PG.	FORM	MATERIALS	COLOR SCHEME
FATHER CHRISTMAS SHELF ENSEMBLE:				
Spiral Garland	23	Garland	(Same as Spiral Garland for Fireplace); woven gold ribbon.	Red/Cream
Gold Leaf Swag	23	Free-form	White mallee eucalyptus sprayed gold.	Gold
Twig Bundles	23	Bouquet	Silver birch twigs sprayed copper.	Copper
CHRISTMAS TABLE SETTING:				
Natural Centerpiece in Wooden Bowl	24	Free	Pinecones; pomegranates; acorns; cinnamon sticks; leaves and pinecones sprayed gold; red ribbon; gold bell.	Brown/Gold/Red
Table Garlands	24	Garland	Evergreen boughs; white bruneia sprigs; pomegranates; acorns sprayed gold; red berries.	Green/White/Red
Naturals in Miniature Flower Pots	24	Free-form	Miniature pine cones; acorns sprayed gold; red berries.	Brown/Gold
Miniature Twig Trees	24	Bouquet	Twigs; acorns and pods sprayed gold; red berries.	Brown/Gold
Candlestick Topiaries	26	Topiary	Hybrid tea roses: deep pink, light pink; white mallee eucalyptus leaves.	Pink/Silver
TABLE ACCENTS:				
Tussie-Mussie	28	Bouquet	Hybrid tea roses: deep pink, magenta; blue salvia; Dusty Miller; lavender; artemisia; teal ribbon; gold cord.	Pink/Lavender/Silver
Vase Bouquet	31	Bouquet	Mop-headed hydrangeas: blue,- peach, cream, light turquoise; white bruneia clusters.	Blue/Peach/Turquoise
BEDROOM ENSEMBLE:				
Headboard Garland	32–33	Garland	Mop-headed hydrangeas: dark cranberry, light pink, cream; roses: white, cream; pink peonies; pink nasturiums; Queen Anne's lace; berries: blue, burgundy, black; rose leaves on branches; avocado-and-pink ribbon. (Entire arrangement: silk.)	Pink/Cream

Winter

WINTER DESIGNS	PG.	FORM	MATERIALS	COLOR SCHEME
Night Table Topiary	32–33	Topiary	Hybrid tea roses, everlastings, yarrow; and ranunculus in yellow; pink hybrid tea roses; rose leaves; sheet moss; green ribbon.	Yellow/Pink
CORNER ACCENT: Basket of Lavender	34	Bouquet	Lavender; lavender ribbon.	Lavender
BATHROOM ENSEMBLE: Wall Garlands	37	Garland	Love-lies-bleeding; rose veronica; top brush; rough thistle grass; protea flat; golden yarrow; peach hybrid tea roses; leucophylla; nigella; lavender; white miniature sunray; peach cockscomb; purple statice; leaves: melaleuca; lemon; sage; marjoram.	Peach/Green
Shelf Garland	37	Garland	Nigella; green chenopodium; globe amaranth; white miniature sunray.	Peach/Green

Decorating with Wreaths, Garlands, and Topiaries

Making a Wreath

CHOOSING THE FRAME

There is a variety of ready-made wreath frames available, each type determined by the material from which it is constructed.

VINE: Found naturally as flexible branches of climbing plants; available with or without bark, and in painted varieties; generally sturdy enough to hold heavy decoration.

DRY-FOAM: A synthetic material found in blocks and in curved or flat rings; can be carved and/or joined together with adhesive tape to form larger frames; generally suited for lightweight decoration and especially good for fresh plant materials when ring is moistened and carefully decorated to avoid crumbling foam.

STRAW: Naturally dried grasses compressed into ring shapes and bound with nylon string; generally suited for moderately heavy materials and decoration attached by floral picks.

WIRE: Flexible and strong, and available in varying gauges; particularly versatile, allowing free-form designs (especially chicken wire); suitable for any weight decoration, from light to very heavy.

MAKING A VINE WREATH FRAME

Materials:
Vine
Pruning shears
Reel wire
Wire cutters

Directions:
1. Cut 6 or 7 equal lengths of vine using pruning shears, keeping in mind that the length of the vine will determine the circumference of the wreath.

2. Bend one vine into a hoop, overlapping and weaving the ends together; secure with reel wire wound around the overlapping vines.

3. Interweave each of the remaining vines, one at a time, tucking in ends behind the main vine and moving around the frame until all lengths are used and the desired thickness is achieved.

4. Remove wire at overlap.

5. Decorate as desired.

MAKING A WIRE WREATH FRAME

Materials:

Medium-gauge stub wire

Floral tape

Wire cutters

Directions:

1. Cut a length of medium-gauge wire using wire cutters, and bend into a hoop, keeping in mind that the length of the wire will determine the circumference of the wreath.

2. Overlap the ends of the wire, twisting to secure.

3. Wind floral tape around the overlap, continuing around the entire circumference of hoop, pulling the floral tape taut and overlapping the edges as you work.

4. Decorate as desired.

MAKING A CHICKEN-WIRE FRAME

(Note: This type of frame filled with moistened moss is very suitable for temporarily supporting fresh plant material.)

Materials:

Moss

Chicken wire

Reel wire

Wire cutters

Directions:

1. Cut a rectangular piece of chicken wire using wire cutters, keeping in mind that the length of the wire will determine the circumference of the wreath.

2. Lay the chicken wire on a flat surface and place a thick column of moss along one edge of the full length of chicken wire.

3. Roll the chicken wire over the moss, forming a tube; lash the length of overlap with reel wire to close.

4. Bend the tube into a hoop, adjusting the chicken wire as needed for a smooth surface; join the ends by stuffing a connecting section of moss across the ends of the tube, lashing the edges together with wire.

5. Bend the sharp edges of wire toward the inside.

6. Decorate as desired.

APPLYING THE DECORATION

To vine wreaths: Use fine-gauge wire or hot glue.

To dry-foam wreaths: Use stub-wire bent into staples, or fine-gauge wire; hot glue can be used on denser dry-foam, but experiment on a small section first to avoid melting the foam.

To straw and wire wreaths: Use floral picks, reel string and wire, and hot glue.

Making a Garland

⚘

Note: Any wire-frame garland can be converted to a wreath by bending the garland into a hoop and twisting the ends to secure.

PREPARING THE PLANT MATERIAL

WIRING THE STEMS AND FLOWER HEADS

Materials:

Plant material, as desired

Medium-gauge stub wire

Optional: hot-glue gun and glue sticks

Directions:

1. To lengthen and strengthen any short or fragile stems, mount each stem on a stub wire by holding one end of the wire under the flower head and winding the wire around and beyond the full length of the stem.

2. For pinecones, twist the stub wire around the bottom collar of the scales, allowing one long end to form a false stem.

3. For flower heads without stems, bend a tiny loop at one end of a stub wire; insert the opposite end of the wire through the center of the flower head, pulling the wire through to the other side; wind stub wire around any available stem to secure and reinforce with hot glue, if necessary.

Decorating with Wreaths, Garlands, and Topiaries

MAKING THE GARLAND

Materials:
Prepared plant material as desired
Fine-gauge reel wire
Floral tape
Medium-gauge stub wire
Wire cutters
Optional: hot-glue gun and glue sticks; ribbon, raffia, or other decoration

Directions:
1. Bind individual bouquets using reel wire, concealing wire with floral tape, if desired; set aside.
2. Cut a length of stub wire using wire cutters, keeping in mind that the length of this wire will determine the length of the finished garland; wind floral tape around the full length of the wire (to prevent bound bouquets from slipping).
3. Form a loop at one end and insert one bouquet into the loop, binding it in place with reel wire.
4. Lay the head of the next bouquet over the stems of the first bouquet, binding in place with reel wire and continuing in same way across the entire garland wire.
5. Conceal the bare end of wire with extra plant material hot-glued in place; add ribbon, raffia, or other decoration, as desired.

Note: When working on a garland design that has a central motif, work the design from each end toward the center, overlapping each newly placed bouquet over the stems of the previously placed bouquet so that the stems are hidden. Using a hot-glue gun, add the flowers and foliage to the center area, then fill in any holes or bare spots. For wider garlands, use braided raffia or a wooden dowel for the base.

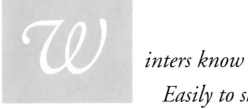

inters know
Easily to shed the snow,
And the untaught Spring is wise
In cowslips and anemones...

—Ralph Waldo Emerson

THE DESIGNS OF SPRING

❧ Floral Spray Door Wreath

❧ Kitchen Ensemble: Potted Topiary, Bouquet, and Wall Garland

❧ Holiday Ensemble: Egg Tree, Bird's Nest, and Railing Garland

❧ Table Topiary

❧ Floral Basket Fireplace Screen

❧ Settee Ensemble: Heart-Shaped Wreath, Vase Bouquet, and Potpourri

❧ Horseshoe-Shaped Clock Garland

❧ Desk Accents: Miniature Topiaries

❧ Hearth Bouquet

❧ Umbrella Topiary

❧ Shelf Accent: Lavender Bouquet

❧ Floor Basket Bouquet

Spring

❧

It seems almost blasphemous to plan springtime floral decorations with anything other than the season's succulent tulip or daffodil, but the truth is that these beautiful flowers do not last long before they wilt, and the cost of replenishing a display is discouraging.

Hence, it is prudent to accent our homes in colors of spring in ways that outlast the fresh but perishable, such as arranging drieds that capture the luminous greens, pale pinks, and bright yellows we associate with the season. The appeal of using dried and preserved flowers like globe amaranth, chenopodium, and roses is that we can prepare bouquets to brighten a corner, plan thick boas to drape mantels and bannisters, or fill several pitchers and place them in a windowsill—and enjoy the colors and promise of spring for months to come.

*F*LORAL SPRAY DOOR WREATH. *Announcing the season of new beginnings is this moss-covered wreath with a crescent of roses, yarrow, yellow cockscomb, and a white blaze of bleached poppy heads on stems, starflowers, ammobium, and edelweiss. Streamers gently cascade along each side of the wreath from a loopy bow in plaid. Because the ribbon is wired at each edge, it can be crinkled and arranged in any position for a dramatic effect.*

THIS PROPERTY HAS BEEN
PLACED ON THE

NATIONAL REGISTER
OF HISTORIC PLACES

BY THE UNITED STATES
DEPARTMENT OF THE INTERIOR

KITCHEN ENSEMBLE: ❧ POTTED TOPIARY—An oversize terra-cotta pot adds crisp contrast and a contemporary feel to this dome-shaped boxwood topiary. The same design can be scaled down to create miniature versions for table decorations or favors. ❧ BOUQUET—A bouquet of hybrid tea roses in varying shades of pink and yellow adds a soft accent to an otherwise hard-edged contemporary setting. ❧ WALL GARLAND—Twigs are interspersed with pink larkspur, white everlastings, and sprigs of boxwood in a slender garland that underlines the majestic eyebrow window of this contemporary kitchen. The scale and position of the garland—ordinarily a fussy detail—are offset by the dominance of a domed boxwood topiary.

*H*OLIDAY ENSEMBLE: ❧ *EGG TREE—In a whimsical application of the bouquet technique, this tree was formed by lashing together pussy willow branches at their bottoms. Inserted into plaster of paris, then allowed to harden, the tree is sturdy enough to hold light decoration. In this case, eggs are "blown out," painted and hung on the branches for Easter. To empty (and thereby lighten) the eggs for hanging, simply blow them out as follows: hold a raw egg upright in one hand and gently but carefully tap a hole the size of a small pearl in the top and bottom of the egg using the point of a very sharp knife. Blow steadily through the top hole until all the raw egg empties through the bottom hole. To decorate, paint with acrylic paint in desired colors; let dry. Hot-glue a loop of ribbon to the top hole and conceal holes with hydrangea florets. Another charming version might be hung with hearts for Valentine's Day or small packages for a child's birthday party.* ❧ *BIRD'S NEST—Based on the technique of converting a garland to a wreath, this nest is given an authentic look by binding twigs, weeds, moss, and sprigs of flowers into a short garland using reel wire; the ends are overlapped, then secured with wire. A layer of sheet moss covers the bottom of the nest, and blown-out eggs cluster in the well.* ❧ *RAILING GARLAND—Running along the ridge of the wainscoting, garlands of pink and yellow roses create a narrow river of color. Made from the broken heads of roses that are hot-glued onto the stiff stalks of dried peonies, these decorations utilize material that might otherwise be discarded.*

When I count my blessings
I count you
twice

To the house of a friend

*T*ABLE TOPIARY. *A hearty miniature boxwood topiary stands in a decorated terra-cotta pot; you can create the same effect of the white, chalky patina by smearing wet plaster of paris on desired areas, then gently sponging off all but a film of sediment.*

*F*LORAL BASKET
FIREPLACE SCREEN.
When the fireplace stands
cold and unused, you can
add bright floral decoration
to relieve the dreariness.
This basket of peonies,
hydrangeas, and branches
was placed in front of a
cardboard screen cut to fit
the fireplace opening and
covered with sheet moss.

SETTEE ENSEMBLE:

❧ HEART-SHAPED WREATH—Ready-made vine wreaths are available in a wide range of shapes and sizes. This one was decorated with silk and dried flowers in pink and yellow to match the surrounding furnishings.

❧ VASE BOUQUET—Silk and dried flowers combine in this delicate bouquet set in a pretty pitcher.

❧ POTPOURRI—Petals from fresh bouquets, corsages, and gardens can be saved in china dishes and mismatched teacups while they air dry. Try enduringly fragrant roses and lavender, to which you can add a few drops of essential oil.

*H*ORSESHOE-SHAPED CLOCK GARLAND. *Thick and full, this garland was fashioned from bundles of caspia accented with flexible stemmed flowers. The remaining flowers were hot-glued into place, as was the shirred wire-edged ribbon in hot pink added to the back of the bent garland . To attach the ribbon to the back of the garland, cut a length of wire-edged ribbon two times the measurement of the perimeter of the garland. Crinkle one long edge of the ribbon, adjusting the gathers so that the ribbon goes around the whole garland. Hot-glue the crinkled edge to the back edge of the garland so that the ribbon shows in front.*

Decorating with Wreaths, Garlands, and Topiaries

$\mathcal{D}$ESK ACCENTS:
❧ MINIATURE
TOPIARIES—Miniature
topiaries made quickly and
easily from heads covered
in sheet moss and impaled
on wooden dowels stand
sentry amid memorabilia
silhouetted against a
light-filled diagonal
Vermont window.

Decorating with Wreaths, Garlands, and Topiaries

HEARTH
BOUQUET. A Federal-style
fireplace is filled to bursting
with pink peonies, roses,
and a vast variety of any
dried materials that suggest
pink. The bouquet is fashioned with a high wall of
flowers in the back, with
succeeding rows of flowers
in descending size. A collar
of white mallee eucalyptus
surrounding the pink
terra-cotta container
finishes the design and
breaks the line of the vessel.

Decorating with Wreaths, Garlands, and Topiaries

UMBRELLA
TOPIARY. *Plump
ranunculus, full-blown
roses, tea roses, and
boxwood sprigs are wired to
create a flexible arch when
bound garland-style onto a
main trunk made of
heavy-gauge wire. The tree
is then set into the neck of
the vase, which has been
plugged with dry-foam.
Because this design is so
lightweight, it is well suited
to more delicate containers.
Never pour plaster of paris
directly into an unprepared
jar, bottle, or vase; the
plaster expands as it sets
and can easily crack the
container.*

*S*HELF ACCENT:
❧ *LAVENDER BOUQUET—*
The fragrance of lavender has long been a favorite for sachets, potpourris, and slender bouquets to slip between the sheets in a linen closet or tuck away in a drawer. Lavender is said to bring luck, so make a few bouquets to last the year and present them as gifts nestled in a basket with other beauty products.

*F*LOOR BASKET
BOUQUET. *Placed on the
floor in front of a window,
this bountiful bouquet of
sea lavender, larkspur,
silver strawberry, sun ray,
poppy seed heads, purple
statice, ammobium, and
leucophylla glows in
silhouette. The choice of
colors was determined by the
strong colors and patterns of
the needlepoint carpet
and painted moldings.
The feathery frame redefines
the contour, lightening an
otherwise compact
arrangement.*

MATERIALS FOR SPRING COLLECTION

This chart offers an overview of this collection by listing the dried materials, the decorative form (wreath, garland, topiary, or bouquet), and the predominant color scheme for each of the designs featured.

SPRING DESIGNS	PG.	FORM	MATERIALS	COLOR SCHEME
Floral Spray Door Wreath	51	Wreath	Hybrid tea roses: cream and yellow; bleached poppy heads; golden yarrow; green gypsum; tansy; cream cockscomb; sea lavender; starflowers, ammobium; boxwood sprigs sprayed green; edelweiss, sheet moss; plaid ribbon; miniature flower pot.	Yellow/White
KITCHEN ENSEMBLE:				
Potted Topiary	52–53	Topiary	Boxwood sprigs sprayed green.	Green
Bouquet	52–53	Bouquet	Hybrid tea roses: yellow, pink, cerise-tinged.	Yellow/Pink
Wall Garland	52–53	Garland	Boxwood sprayed green; pink larkspur; white everlastings; twigs.	Green/Pink/White
HOLIDAY ENSEMBLE:				
Egg Tree	55	Bouquet	Pussy willow branches; sheet moss; eggs; hydrangea florets; striped ribbon.	Brown/Pastels
Bird's Nest	55	Wreath	Twigs; sheet moss; sprigs of golden yarrow, pepperberries, caspia, tansy; hydrangea florets; weeds; eggs; turquoise ribbon.	Green/Brown/ Yellow/Pink
Railing Garland	55	Garland	Hybrid tea roses: yellow, pink, cream; peony stems.	Yellow/Pink

SPRING DESIGNS	PG.	FORM	MATERIALS	COLOR SCHEME
Table Topiary	57	Topiary	Boxwood sprigs sprayed green; sheet moss.	Green
Floral Basket	58–59	Bouquet	Peonies: light pink, dark pink; mop-headed hydrangeas: cream peach; pink hybrid tea roses; white gyp; edelweiss; white mallee eucalyptus; lemon leaves dyed pink; wild oat grass; twigs; slender branches; sheet moss; ribbon.	Pink/Cream
SETTEE ENSEMBLE: Heart-Shaped Wreath	60–61	Wreath	Grapevine; golden yarrow; everlastings: gold, yellow; silk flowers: pink, yellow.	Yellow/Pink
Vase Bouquet	60–61	Bouquet	Hybrid tea roses: yellow, pink, dark pink; yellow everlastings; silk flowers: dark pink, light pink, yellow; white.	Yellow/Pink
Potpourri	60–61	Free	Rose petals	Pink
Horseshoe-Shaped Clock Garland	63	Garland	Linen caspia; bleached gypsum white sunray; hybrid tea roses: wine, pink, cream; edelweiss; white ranunculus; pink larkspur; pink cockscomb; hydrangea florets; purple statice; dark-green eucalyptus sprigs. hot pink ribbon.	Pink/White/Purple
DESK ACCENTS: Miniature Topiaries	64–65	Topiary	Moss: sheet, bun, sphagnum; stick; teal blue ribbon.	Green
Hearth Bouquet	66–67	Bouquet	Peonies: light pink, dark pink, dark magenta; hybrid tea roses: light pink, dark pink, wine; rattail statice; love-lies-bleeding; anise hyssop; pink larkspur; delphinium; suveroni;artemisia; purple salvia; white mallee eucalyptus leaves	Pink

SPRING DESIGNS	PG.	FORM	MATERIALS	COLOR SCHEME
Umbrella Topiary	68–69	Topiary	Hybrid tea roses: pink, dark pink, yellow; yellow ranunculus; boxwood sprigs; moss: bun and sphagnum.	Yellow/Pink
SHELF ACCENT: Lavender Bouquet	70–71	Bouquet	Lavender; moss green ribbon.	Lavender
Floor Basket Bouquet	72–73	Bouquet	Sea lavender; larkspur; pink and blue; silver strawberry; sun-ray; poppy seed heads; lemon mint; purple statice; ammobium; leucophylla; caspia; artemisia.	White/Pink/Blue

Making a Topiary

❧

PREPARING THE HEAD

TYPE A: Dry-foam block
Materials:
Dry-foam block
Sharp knife
Optional: narrow adhesive tape

Directions: For round head:
1. Sculpt a sphere from a block of dry-foam using a sharp knife to slice away the corners until a ball is formed.
2. For a larger sphere, tape two blocks of dry foam securely together; sculpt sphere of desired size, following Step 1.

TYPE B: Wire and moss
Materials:
Chicken wire
Wire cutters
Dry-foam scraps
Spray adhesive
Sheet moss
Fine-gauge wire on reel

Directions:
1. Cut a rectangularly shaped piece of chicken wire using wire cutters so that the length of the piece is slightly larger than the desired circumference of the sphere.
2. Place the piece of chicken wire on a flat surface, and pile dry-foam scraps into a mound in the center.
3. Lift one side of the chicken wire up and over the mound, adding more dry-foam scraps until a sphere of desired size is formed.
4. Lift the other side of the chicken wire over mound, overlapping the first side and bending in sharp ends.
5. Continue bending and flattening the edges of the chicken wire until the sphere is the desired shape and size.

6. Spray a large, unbroken section of sheet moss with adhesive and press onto chicken wire; secure moss in place by winding reel wire around the sphere.

7. Continue spraying and binding sections of sheet moss until entire sphere is covered.

WHEN SELECTING THE HEAD FOR THE TOPIARY, CONSIDER THE FOLLOWING:

Dry-foam heads hold only lighter-weight material.

Chicken-wire heads are suitable for heavier decoration.

Chicken-wire covered with plastic wrap, then covered with sheet moss that has been moistened, allows for the use of fresh flowers and foliage.

Chicken wire is versatile and can be bent into cones and other shapes of any size.

CONSTRUCTING THE BASIC TOPIARY

PREPARING THE BASE

Materials:

Coping saw

Straight, firm stick or tree branch

Flower pot

Dry-foam scraps

Floral clay

Plaster of paris powder

Head of topiary

Adhesive tape (for dry-foam sphere) or stub wires (for wire- and-moss sphere)

1. Using a coping saw, cut a topiary trunk from a straight, firm stick or tree branch in proportion to the overall height of the topiary; set aside.

2. Line a flower pot with scraps of dry-foam, securing in place with floral clay. (The dry-foam will provide a cushion and prevent the drying plaster from cracking the pot.)

3. Mix a batch of plaster of paris, following package directions. Fill the flower pot 2/3 full, and insert the topiary trunk in the center of the mixture, making certain the trunk is centered and straight when viewed from all angles.

4. Add more plaster to fill pot; hold trunk in place until secure.

5. Prepare the head of the topiary in proportion to its overall height and contour, following the directions on the previous page.

6. To affix the head onto the trunk:

For dry-foam sphere: Impale the head on the trunk and secure in place using narrow strips of adhesive tape crisscrossed over the top and underside of the sphere, and wound around the trunk.

For wire-and-moss sphere: Impale the head on the trunk and secure in place using stub wires threaded through underside of the sphere and wound around the trunk.

7. Decorate the head and conceal plaster as desired, or set pot into a larger ornamental container.

DECORATING THE TOPIARY HEAD

Materials:

Cover material:

Moss (i.e., sphagnum, bun, or sheet)

Dried flowers and foliage

Silk flowers and foliage

Note: The addition of dried and silk materials will make the head one-third to one-half larger in circumference than the unadorned head.

Spray adhesive

Sheet moss

Floral pins or fine-gauge stub wires

Floral tape

Fine-gauge reel wire

Medium-gauge stub wires, if stems need to be lengthened or strengthened

Directions:

To cover topiary with moss:

1. Apply spray adhesive on wrong side of an unbroken section of moss and press the moss into place on the topiary head; if necessary, further secure moss with floral pins or fine-gauge stub wire bent into a staple shape and pushed through moss into the dry-foam. Or wind reel wire around the sphere.

2. Continue spraying and pressing moss into place on the head until surface is covered or in the desired pattern.

To cover topiary head with silk or dried flowers or foliage:

1. Reinforce and/or lengthen the stems if necessary, following directions on page 44.

2. Push the stems into the topiary head until covered or in the desired pattern.

NOTE:

When decorating head with boxwood, consider preparing your own by cutting live branches and spraying the entire branch with green paint; you may use acrylic or oil-base following manufacturer's directions. The coat of paint will preserve the foliage. Or, spruce up faded leaves with a light, overall coat of paint.

T he silent orchard aisles
are sweet
With the smell of ripening fruit.
Through the sere grass, in shy retreat,
Flutter, at coming feet...

—W. D. Howells

THE DESIGNS OF SUMMER

❧ Door Wreath

❧ Kitchen Ensemble: Door Wreath and Window Garland

❧ Pantry Ensemble: Miniature Wreaths, Basket Bouquet,

   China Closet Bouquet, and Cake Garland

❧ Hat Garlands

❧ Door Garlands

❧ Porch Ensemble: Maypole Topiaries

❧ Portico Ensemble: Bouquet Centerpiece and Napkin Rings

❧ Ring Topiary

❧ Wagon Herb Garland

❧ Monogram Garland

Summer

꘎

It is summer. There is moisture and sunshine and a fragrance of roses in the air. This is the season to look toward your garden for flowers and foliage that will add bursts of color to any area, indoors or out. Buttercup yellow, poppy red, sapphire blue—all these rich primary colors can be found in dried materials as well.

The joy of summer is due in large part to the vastly broader palette of flowers as well as the fact that it's the perfect time to begin harvesting fresh flowers at their peak for drying yourself. And drying does not have to be done on a large scale: Save the flowers you received from a guest; cut two or three cabbage roses from a bush; buy a bouquet just for drying. Many fresh flowers and vines, such as late summer's hydrangeas and statice, can be allowed to dry in the containers where they stood fresh. Also, do not hesitate to mix live foliage in muted shades with preserved flowers. Silvery green eucalyptus leaves combined with dark pink roses and white everlastings look splendid when bunched in small vases or used as tussie-mussies or at table settings. You will soon find yourself collecting all varieties of natural materials for your own designs.

*K*ITCHEN ENSEMBLE: ❧ DOOR WREATH—*The season's bounty is displayed in this wreath made from a base of white mallee eucalyptus branches. Do not feel compelled to pack decoration all around the perimeter of the circle. Consider, instead, a crescent of flowers and foliage on only a portion of the wreath.* ❧ WINDOW GARLAND—*(Overleaf) Made of fresh foliage, the garland is allowed to air dry in place, thereby rounding the sharp turns at the corners of the window without breaking. The flowers are a mixture of fresh and dried secured in place by inserting the stems in between the boughs of eucalyptus and English ivy.*

Decorating with Wreaths, Garlands, and Topiaries

*P*ANTRY ENSEMBLE (Pages 88–89): ❧ MINIATURE WREATHS—A trio of miniature wreaths, each made by sewing through the heads of safflowers with wire, hangs in a row along the doors of an old-fashioned Hoosier. Small patchwork hearts rest in the centers of the wreaths.

❧ BASKET BOUQUET—Tucked into a woven basket are field grasses and weeds routinely collected on leisurely walks. ❧ CHINA CLOSET BOUQUET—Atop of the quinessentially American oak china cabinet is a basket of dried caspia, a popular dried foliage available in abundance in all colors (since it is dyed) and a perfect filler material due to its natural volume. Resting on top of the Hoosier is a collection of favorite folk-art animals, along with bundles of dried grasses and decorative foliage. The bouquet of wheat adds just the right touch to this country still life. ❧ CAKE GARLAND—Best decorated with live blossoms, this homemade layered chocolate cake is decorated with small rosebuds and sprigs of other garden flowers. Be certain to choose flowers that are safe to decorate food; many varieties are toxic. Check with a reputable authority before applying any decoration. Never use preserved drieds!

*H*AT GARLANDS: ❧ ON LEFT—A dainty garland of dark-pink everlastings and globe amaranth arches around the crown of an old straw hat. The design appears monochromatic until you get closer and see the subtle shadings. ❧ ON RIGHT—A random arrangement of saved flower heads and sprigs reveals a charming medallion of summer color on the front brim of a child's straw hat. Each of these designs can be a study for a larger piece, of course; you can quickly assess color and scale by practicing on smaller projects.

$\mathcal{D}$OOR GARLANDS.

These untamed-looking floral "sketches" are garlands made from dried long-bladed grass mixed with flowers and light foliage that appear to have been collected in the wild. Actually, the white, pink, and lime green are added with sprigs of everlasting silver foliage, globe amaranth, and chenopodium. The raffia bow suggests hot summer days in the country. These garlands can be made to hang over doorways, place along the center of a table, or pile into willow baskets. By using foliage gathered on walks, you can amass a variety of natural materials while on vacation.

*P*ORCH ENSEMBLE: ❧ *MAYPOLE TOPIARIES*—*Preparing for guests during the summer is so satisfying because you can use fresh flowers in your table designs—just remember to provide a base that can absorb water and is strong enough to hold live plant material. These maypole topiaries are made in identical fashion; the only difference is in the scale and proportion of the wreath to the stem and container. Each wreath base is made from dry-foam stuffed tubes of chicken wire made into rings, then covered with moss and moistened before inserting the plant material. Decorating with fresh flowers is always an appealing, if temporary, extravagance.*

Decorating with Wreaths, Garlands, and Topiaries

$\mathcal{B}$OUQUET
CENTERPIECE.
The focal point of this

elegant table set for brunch

is the lush centerpiece with

peonies in varying pinks,

clusters of tea roses, and

stems of fragrant lavender.

Decorating with Wreaths, Garlands, and Topiaries

*N*APKIN RINGS. *Napkin rings made from dried red roses, white everlastings, and dusty-green eucalyptus leaves echo the elegant theme of the Bouquet Centerpiece.*

Decorating with Wreaths, Garlands, and Topiaries

R*ING TOPIARY.*

A peeled willow wreath in a

twisted rope pattern

provides the head for this

ring topiary. Decorated with

dried oranges and purple

statice, the head is wired to

a dowel and inserted into

an enamel pot filled with

plaster of paris and allowed

to set. When completely dry

and hard, the surface of the

plaster is covered with buns

of bright-orange browneii.

*W*AGON HERB
GARLAND. *A fragrant
and useful garland of
oregano, anise, and marjoram decorates the rim of an
antique wagon; later it will
be brought into the kitchen
and used to flavor soups and
freshly baked bread. You
can use garlic to decorate the
garland, as well as everlastings to add color.*

Decorating with Wreaths, Garlands, and Topiaries

$\mathcal{M}$ONOGRAM GARLAND. *A long garland made from a wired base of sphagnum moss is bent into an S and decorated with roses in pink and yellow using hot glue. Tendrils made from covered wire add balance and elegance to the design.*

MATERIALS FOR SUMMER COLLECTION

This chart offers an overview of this collection by listing the dried materials, the decorative form (wreath, garland, topiary, or bouquet), and the predominant color scheme for each of the designs featured.

SUMMER DESIGNS	PG.	FORM	MATERIALS	COLOR SCHEME
Door Wreath	85	Wreath	Larkspur; delphinium; blue statice; ranunculus: yellow and white; pink globe amaranth; lachnostachys; dark pink everlastings; lime green gypsum; white mallee eucalyptus.	Multicolored
KITCHEN ENSEMBLE: Door Wreath	86–87	Wreath	(Same as above.)	Multicolored
Window Garland	86–87	Garland	Same as above; edelweiss; ivy.	Multicolored
PANTRY ENSEMBLE: Miniature Wreaths	88–89	Wreath	Safflower heads lightly sprayed gold.	Green/Gold
Basket Bouquet	88–89	Bouquet	Field grasses; weeds; ammobium.	Pink/Gray
Pantry Top	88–89	Varied	Bunches: safflower Dusty Miller; wheat bouquet; pomegranates.	Green/Cream/Red
China Closet Bouquet	88–89	Bouquet	Caspia.	Gray
Cake Garland*	88–89	Free-form	Hybrid tea roses: light pink, dark pink; sunray; edelweiss; purple statice; ivy leaves, rose leaves; pink striped ribbon.	Pink/White/Purple

* DO NOT USE PRESERVED DRIED FLOWERS OR FOLIAGE WITH FOOD; IT IS TOXIC. CHOOSE DRIED FLORALS THAT YOU HAVE CONFIRMED ARE SAFE FOR USE WITH FOOD!

SUMMER DESIGNS	PG.	FORM	MATERIALS	COLOR SCHEME
HAT GARLANDS:				
On Left	91	Garland	Everlastings: dark pink, light pink; globe amaranth; boxwood sprigs; teal blue ribbon.	Pink
On Right	91	Garland	Blue mop-headed hydrangeas; hybrid tea roses: light pink, dark pink, wine, cream; white ranunculus; sprigs: purple statice, larkspur, pink and blue larkspur; delphinium, boxwood; black velvet ribbon.	Pink/Blue/White
Door Garlands	92–93	Garland	Pink globe amaranth; green gypsum; artemisia; sea lavender; grass; raffia.	Pink/White/Green
PORCH ENS EMBLE: Maypole Topiaries				
On Left	94	Topiary/ Wreath	Live pink carnations; fern; sheet moss; blue and white striped ribbon.	Pink
On Right	94	Topiary/ Wreath	Pink carnations; purple statice; sheet moss; variegated ribbon.	Pink/Purple
Bouquet Centerpiece	96–97	Bouquet	Peonies: light pink, dark pink; hybrid tea roses: dark pink, light pink, pink-tinged cream; lavender; blue salvia.	Pink
Napkin Rings	98–99	Free-form	Red hybrid tea roses; white everlastings; purple larkspur; white mallee eucalyptus; mint green ribbon.	Red/White
Ring Topiary	100–101	Topiary/ Wreath	Oranges; purple statice; safflower; orange browneii.	Orange/Purple
Wagon Herb Garland	102–103	Garland	Herbs: oregano, anise, marjoram; tansy; everlastings: dark pink, gold, orange, rust; purple rose veronica; magenta globe amaranth; peony leaves; berries; bird.	Gold/Yellow/Purple

SUMMER DESIGNS	PG.	FORM	MATERIALS	COLOR SCHEME
Monogram Garland	103-104	Garland	Hybrid tea roses: light pink, dark pink, cream, yellow; blue mop-head hydrangea florets; pepper berries; rose leaves; sphagnum moss.	Yellow/Pink

Making a Bouquet

The term "bouquet" refers to floral arrangements that are formed by gathering bunches of material together and securing them at their stems as well as to arrangements with stems that have been inserted into a common base of dry-foam or other holding material, or a vase.

NOTE: To antique a terra-cotta flower pot, use a sponge to lightly apply blotches of acrylic paint in white, green, and black, overlapping each previous color when dry. When all layers are completely dry, scrape the surface with a sharp knife to create a mottled look.

PREPARING THE CONTAINER

Materials:
Dry-foam to fill inside of container
Sharp knife
Floral clay and a plastic prong for bowls; medium-gauge stub wire for baskets
Narrow adhesive tape
Sphagnum moss or some cover material to conceal foam

Directions:
1. Place the block of dry-foam over the bottom of the container, pressing down to form an indentation pattern.
2. Shape the foam with sharp knife, using the indentation pattern as a guide and following the general contour of the container for a tight fit.
3. Lay a second block of foam on the first if a mound higher than the container is desired.
4. Secure the foam in the container as follows:

For bowl or ceramic container: Place gobs of floral clay at even intervals across the bottom of the container, then press a plastic prong on a gob in the center. Impale the foam on the prong, then crisscross two lengths of adhesive tape tightly over the foam block, securing the ends to the outside of the bowl.

For basket: Follow directions for a bowl or ceramic container, but secure the ends of the tape by threading them through the cane at the opposite sides of the basket and allowing the ends to stick back on themselves.

ARRANGING THE PLANT MATERIAL

There is a lot of latitude when it comes to arranging any bouquet; the following technique allows you to add single flowers or leaves, or clusters of chosen drieds one piece at a time. You can assess your design with respect to size, proportion, and color as you work, and you can easily pull out an undesired selection.

It's important to plan a design that fits the display space, to choose a container in proportion to the overall design and substantial enough to hold a heavy bouquet, and to vary the sizes and textures of the plant material to create design interest.

Materials:
Dried and/or silk flowers and foliage
Prepared container
Stub wires
Floral tape
Wire cutters
Hot-glue gun and glue sticks

Directions:
Note: Reinforce and/or lengthen the stems of any plant material, if necessary following the directions on page 44.

For an arrangement that will be seen from one side only:
1. Insert a row of plant material, one stem at a time or in wired bunches, in a soft fan shape at the back of the container.
2. Work forward, adding flowers of varying textures and shapes in rough lines, decreasing the height of each new row so as not to obscure the flower heads in back.
3. Step away from the arrangement to get an overall sense of the design as you work; rearrange any flowers, clustering any components to create a stronger design statement.
4. When satisfied with the arrangement of the basic floral components, add foliage to fill in the empty

spaces, placing some shorter-stemmed foliage near the front to conceal any bare stems and to break the line of the container. Augment sparsely flowered stems using hot glue to attach extra flower heads or leaves, as desired.

For an arrangement that will be seen from all sides:
1. Insert the plant material into the center of the prepared container, adding flowers and foliage so that it emanates from the center in a soft dome shape.
2. Vary the texture and shape of the plant material, mixing spike-shaped components with plump and wispy selections.
3. Allow the natural curve of the stems to dictate their placement, with stronger curves being placed at the front so they break the line of the container.
4. Fill in spaces, inserting the stems of plant material at low angles if the arrangement is to be seen from below.
5. Use a hot-glue gun to attach extra flower heads or foliage to sparse plant material, as desired.

COLLECTING CONES, PODS, AND GRASSES

Cones, pods, and grasses can be found in great abundance and add color and shape to arrangements. Although it is ecologically wise to collect your finds after they have fallen to the ground, it is also possible to collect samples from the tree. Wild grasses and weeds can be snipped from their stems, so travel with a sharp pair of scissors on your walks in autumn. Take small bouquets of grass or weeds, for example, from different clumps, being careful not to rip the plants by their root. Be aware of protected species, like dune grass, that are illegal to cut. However, you will find that grasses grow in abundance in fields and along roadsides and can be collected with a clear conscience. Because grasses tend to shrivel unevenly while drying, press the blades in absorbent paper to maintain their shape; if you prefer the soft twists and curls of dried grass, dry the grass in a newspaper-lined cardboard box until ready to use.

DRYING YOUR OWN PLANT MATERIAL
THE AIR-DRY METHOD

Although there are elaborate (and expensive) methods for drying flowers and plant material, the easiest and most effective way to preserve their natural color, texture, and shape is to air dry them. Simply collect a small bunch of desired flowers or foliage and hang it upside down in a dry, cool, dimly lit place, such as an attic eave or spare closet. Direct sunlight will fade color, and moisture will encourage mold to form. It is best to strip some of the leaves to keep from trapping moisture when stems are placed together in the bunch. Binding the stems with a rubber band keeps them together as they dry and shrink. Drying time will be determined by the thickness of the stems, leaves, and flower heads, but it generally takes a week or two. Properly dried material will feel like paper.

Certain plant material (like leaves and moss) can be dried laying flat on absorbent paper or on window screens; inserting the stems of heavy-headed flowers and plants into chicken wire allows the individual heads to maintain their shape. However, certain flowers such as hydrangeas dry best standing in an inch or two of water. You may wish to consult the bibliography for books that offer a broader discussion of other drying methods as well as techniques for growing, picking, and preserving dried materials.

CARING FOR YOUR DRIED-FLOWER CREATIONS

It would be lovely to think that after all your time and effort, your dried-flower creations would endure year after year. But the fact is that arrangements made of dried and preserved materials are fragile and subject to breaking and fading, though you can prolong their life by keeping them away from direct sunlight and humidity and by not moving them too much.

However, there are other ways to capitalize on their intrinsic beauty as they age. The soft, faded colors of roses are compatible with arrangements that are Victorian or romantic in style. You can enhance the antique look by adding a faded or pale-colored ribbon to further bring out the muted shades.

You might also consider recycling the flowers or flower heads when an arrangement is no longer intact. You can add the salvageable elements to new arrangements or simply create a miniature version of the original. Consider brushing on a dusting of color with powdered eye shadow or blush.

If the arrangement is faded but otherwise intact, try spray painting the entire piece; a garland of leaves sprayed gold or copper around a mirror adds elegance during the holidays. Finally, when the arrangement is no longer attractive, consider using the flower petals for potpourri. You will discover ways to work with all the materials and develop new techniques and effective shortcuts of your own. Most important, you will develop the skills to create original designs to complement your own home decor or to give as unique gifts.

Gold of a ripe oat straw, gold of a southwest moon
Canada thistle blue and flimmering larkspur blue,
Tomatoes shining in the October sun with red hearts,
Shining five and six in a row on a wooden fence...

—Carl Sandburg

THE DESIGNS OF AUTUMN

- ❧ Billowy Door Wreath

- ❧ Dining Room Ensemble: Sideboard Fan Topiary and Centerpiece Bouquet

- ❧ Foyer; Harvest Topiary and Stairway Vine

- ❧ Bouquet in Antique Box

- ❧ Oak Leaf Topiary

- ❧ Arched Wall Garland

- ❧ Wild Bouquet in Carpenter's Box

- ❧ Wheat Bouquet

- ❧ Van Gogh Vase Bouquet

- ❧ Herbal Bouquets

- ❧ Dome Topiary

Autumn

❦

Presenting its own splendid palette and a fullness of nature's bounty, autumn offers us flaming oranges, burnt browns, and golds. This season is a particularly rewarding time for walks through the countryside; cones and pods, ornamental grasses, and weeds are now abundant; hydrangeas, everlastings, autumn roses, and goldenrod can be harvested and hung to dry. There is "autumn in everything," as Robert Browning said, and this feeling of abundance flourishes in us as well.

The rich colors and textures find expression in the velvet and brocade of our furnishings and in the lush decorations of Thanksgiving. In an atmosphere of warmth and sharing, our sense of well-being grows; how delightful to come in from the cold to a living room warmed by a fire and fragrant with spices and fruit. Reflecting the change of season are the wreaths we hang, the garlands we swag, and the topiaries and bouquets we display, keeping the shorter days and the sudden snap in the air from lowering our spirits.

*B*ILLOWY DOOR WREATH. *Plump mop-headed hydrangeas in cream and light green cover the entire surface of a straw-base wreath; though secured with wire "staples," each hydrangea head could have been hot-glued in place as well. Hydrangea is not as fragile as it appears and is a frequently used filler for large areas.*

$\mathcal{D}$INING ROOM ENSEMBLE: ❧ SIDEBOARD FAN TOPIARY—(*previous page and above*) *A fan-shaped topiary with a scalloped arch echoes the color scheme of the dining room; velvety cockscomb in magenta-tinged pink and cream is outlined by rows of blue statice, and a broad crescent of yellow tansy and yarrow finishes the lower section. This topiary head was formed by cutting a fan shape from heavy cardboard and hot-gluing each row of dried materials, moving from top to bottom. A dowel trunk connects the head to the base, a small but heavy antique urn.*

Centerpiece Bouquet (pages 120–121 and above)—This stunning "bouquet" is made by placing

clusters of flowers, fruits, and pods mounted on stub wires into blocks of dry-foam, which are built into

a dome and secured to a terra-cotta flower pot with adhesive tape. To insure a balance it is important

to choose a heavy container.

Decorating with Wreaths, Garlands, and Topiaries

*F*OYER: ❧ *HARVEST TOPIARY—*
The focal point of this foyer is the loose and
scraggly contour of faded foliage and weeds
arranged in the topiary head; the soft color-
ing complements the "moldy" terra-cotta pot
and the trunk lightly wrapped in sphagnum
moss. The federal blue–painted woodwork
further enhances the wheat colors. To create
the chalky white mold, paint the outside of
the pot with natural yogurt months ahead
of time, and actual mold will be encouraged
to grow. The original design was created by
Village Flowers; silk leaves and goldenrod as
well other dried foliage have been added to
plump up the contour. ❧ *STAIRWAY*
VINE—The trail of silk grape leaves inter-
spersed with goldenrod provides a delicate
accent and pleasing interruption to an
otherwise linear composition.

$\mathcal{B}$OUQUET IN
ANTIQUE BOX. *The
overall contour of this
arrangement depends on the
unity of all the design elements. The rectangle of the
box is counterbalanced by
the compact dome of flowers,
a framework of caspia
relieves the hard edge of the
top arch, and the uneven
arrangement of materials
breaks the line of the box.
Textural interest is achieved
by mixing smooth-petaled
flowers, like roses and
ranunculus, with dotty-
headed yarrow and
hydrangeas. By interweav-
ing leaves, stems, twigs, and
seed heads, even greater textural variation is achieved.*

Decorating with Wreaths, Garlands, and Topiaries

OAK LEAF
TOPIARY. *The highly
detailed character of the leaf
of miniature pin oak is sim-
plified by the soft curve of
the dark verdigris urn. This
topiary-style design requires
that the "tree" head be prepared following the directions for a garland, with
each tier using successively
longer stems of oak until the
desired size is achieved.*

$\mathcal{A}$RCHED
WALL GARLAND. *One of
the few pieces that use silk
flowers, this wall garland
capitalizes on the exquisite
and authentic-looking
branches of silk bittersweet.
Because bittersweet is such a
vibrant and prized addition
to many autumnal arrange-
ments, it is highly sought
after. Unfortunately, it does
not grow in many regions,
but the silk variation is a
fine substitute. Combined
with birch or any other type
of branch having a small
leaf, bittersweet adds a
splash of orange dots,
enhancing the rustic beauty
and textural interest of the
design.*

Decorating with Wreaths, Garlands, and Topiaries

WILD BOUQUET
IN CARPENTER'S BOX.
*Probably the easiest bouquet to
arrange, this wildly textured
and color-contrasted mixture of
cream and purple flowers was
made by laying a foundation of
dry-foam along the full length
of the bottom of an antique
carpenter's toolbox and
inserting armloads of dried
material in an arched spray.
A box of this size requires a
lot of material, so you may
wish instead to fill a smaller
container using the same
configuration.*

132

$\mathcal{W}$HEAT
BOUQUET. Inspired by the
sheaves of wheat found in mown
fields, this sleekly beautiful and
compact bouquet of golden
wheat is the perfect accent for
an entry table, small corner
shelf, or cabinet top. The stems
have been bundled carefully into
a central core and bound together with waxed string; layer upon
layer of wheat stems are added
and bound in place, allowing
the heads to form a fan-shaped
dome. The stems will naturally
fan out and twist slightly. A
French wired ribbon in deep
teal encircles the bouquet, and a
medallion of pot marigold and
eucalyptus leaves adds a splash
of sunshine.

135

$\mathcal{V}$AN GOGH
VASE BOUQUET. The
color orange, expressed in
great textural variety, pulls
together this sumptuous
bouquet in a ceramic vase
decorated Van Gogh–style.
Golden yarrow, pot
marigold, and everlastings
in burnt orange, yellow,
and rust are glorious harvest
colors that combine to create
dramatic interest and
country charm. The small
bouquets are of sage,
marjoram, and oregano
picked fresh and allowed to
dry "in situ."

Decorating with Wreaths, Garlands, and Topiaries

$\mathcal{D}$OME TOPIARY.

This aristocratic topiary is made with a dome-shaped globe of purple statice and a traditional terra-cotta flowerpot wrapped in sheet moss; the head and base are connected with a trunk of birch accentuated by a parallel length of grapevine. The appeal of this topiary lies in the surprising harmony of its bold colors and straightforward geometry.

MATERIALS FOR AUTUMN COLLECTION

This chart offers an overview of this collection by listing the dried materials, the decorative form (wreath, garland, topiary, or bouquet), and the predominant color scheme for each of the designs featured.

AUTUMN DESIGNS	PG.	FORM	MATERIALS	COLOR SCHEME
Billowy Door Wreath	119	Wreath	Mop-headed hydrangeas: cream, light green.	Cream
DINING ROOM ENSEMBLE: Sideboard Fan Topiary	120–21	Topiary	Cockscomb: dark pink, cream; hybrid tea roses: yellow and pink; tansy; golden yarrow; blue statice; moss; lime green ribbon.	Pink/Yellow
Sideboard Centerpiece Bouquet	123	Bouquet	Mop-headed hydrangeas: cream, peach; cockscomb: cream, pink; hybrid tea roses: light pink, dark pink, cream, magenta, light yellow; purple statice; golden yarrow; tansy; wild bunny tails; goldenrod; oranges; seed pods; nuts; freeze-dried fruit: apple slices, pear slices; Silk grape clusters; silk magenta peonies; antique cord and tassel.	Multi-Colored
FOYER: Harvest Topiary	124–25	Topiary	Faded boxwood sprigs, goldenrod; lemon leaves; sheet and lace moss; wood shavings; grapevine; sphagnum moss; artificial peaches; silk leaves in vine.	Cream/Orange
Stairway Vine	124–25	Garland	Silk grape leaves; live ivy vine; goldenrod.	Gold
Bouquet in Antique Box	126	Bouquet	Hybrid tea roses: yellow, cream, light pink, dark pink; goldenrod; golden yarrow; yellow ranunculus; yellow de solei; purple statice; blue larkspur; blue salvia; purple mop-headed hydrangeas; lime green gypsum; magenta globe amaranth; magenta Kansas City gay feather; linen caspia; anise hyssop; eucalyptus leaves; beech leaves; pods; seed heads; oranges; pinecones; grape vine; Silk clusters of grapes.	Yellow/Orange/Purple/Pink

AUTUMN DESIGNS	PG.	FORM	MATERIALS	COLOR SCHEME
Oak Leaf Topiary	128–29	Bouquet/ Topiary	Miniature pin oak dyed deep copper; sphagnum moss.	Copper
Arched Wall Garland	130–31	Garland	Beech tree branches; silver birch twigs sprayed copper; Silk bittersweet.	Brown/Orange
Wild Bouquet in Carpenter's Box	132–33	Bouquet	Wild grasses; snow gum leaves; purple bunny tails; light and dark purple larkspur; cream hybrid tea roses; cream star flowers; gray caspia; white mallee eucalyptus leaves; ribbons: light green and variegated.	Cream/Purple
Wheat Bouquet	134–35	Bouquet	Wheat; white mallee eucalyptus; de solei; teal ribbon.	Cream
Van Gogh Vase Bouquet	136–37	Bouquet	Golden yarrow; pot marigold; safflower; everlastings: gold, orange, yellow, rust; orange or browneii; sage.	Gold/Yellow/Orange
Herbal Bouquets	136–37	Bouquet	Sage; majoram; oregano.	Green/Purple
Dome Topiary	138–39	Topiary	Purple statice; sheet moss; sphagnum moss; grapevine; purple ribbon.	Purple/Green

THE SOURCE DIRECTORY

RETAIL STORES, CRAFTS SHOPS, AND GARDEN CENTERS

The following retail stores, crafts shops, and garden centers offer a wide selection of dried flowers and herbs, from supplies to ready-made arrangements and decorations.

Afton Grove
1000 Torrey Pines Road
La Jolla, CA 92037
(619) 456 2200
Dried flowers, ready-made wreaths, garlands, and topiaries; mail-order service available.

Aphrodesia
264 Bleeker Street
New York, NY 10014
(212) 989 6440
Dried flowers and supplies to make wreaths, garlands, and topiaries.

Arts & Flowers
54 West 74th Street
New York, NY 10023
(212) 874 4851
Custom work in silk and dried flowers; ready-made arrangements available.

Bittersweet Hill Nurseries
1274 Governor's Bridge Road
Davidsonville, MD 21035
(410) 798 0231
Ready-made wreaths, garlands, and topiaries, and some dried flowers and floral-arts supplies.

Caprilands Herb Farm
Silver Street
Coventry, CT 06238
(203) 742 7244
Ready-made culinary and herb wreaths.

Catnip Acres Herb Nursery
67 Christian Street
Oxford, CT 06483
(203) 888 5649
Dried flowers and herbs, ready-made wreaths, garlands, and topiaries, and floral-arts supplies.

Courtyards
3980 Main Road
Tiverton, RI 02878
(401) 624 8682
Dried flowers, ready-made wreaths, garlands, and topiaries, and some floral-arts supplies.

Cricket Hill Herb Farm Ltd.
Glen street
Rowley, MA 01969
(508) 948 2818
Some dried flowers, potted herbs and potpourri materials.

Dean & DeLuca
560 Broadway
New York, NY 10012
(212) 431 1691
Culinary wreaths.

Dillworthtown Country Store
275 Burton's Bridge Road
West Chester, PA 19382
(215) 399 0560
Some floral-arts supplies.

Flower Fantasiland
10 Robinson Avenue
East Patchogue, NY
(516) 475 2059
Dried flowers and floral-arts supplies.

Flowers Forever
311 East 61st Street
New York, NY 10021
(212) 308 0088
Dried flowers, ready-made wreaths, garlands, and topiaries, floral-arts supplies; accepts custom orders.

Galerie Felix Flower
968 Lexington Avenue
New York, NY 10021
(212) 772 7701
Dried and preserved flowers, ready-made wreaths, garlands, and topiaries, and floral-arts supplies; accepts custom orders; mail-order service available.

Gilbertie's Herb Garden
7 Sylvan Lane
Westport, CT 06880
(203) 227 4175
Dried flowers and dried herbs, ready-made wreaths, garlands, and live topiaries, and floral-arts supplies; mail-order service available.

Griffin's
5109 Vickrey Chapel Road
Greensboro, N.C. 27407
(919) 454 3362
Highly specialized floral arrangements; custom orders accepted.

Hedgehog Hill Farm
RFD 2, Box 2010
Buckfield, ME 04220
(207) 388 2341
Dried flowers, ready-made wreaths, and supplies.

Herb Country Gifts and Collectibles
63 Leonard Street
Belmont Center, MA 02178
(617) 489 1982
Dried flowers, ready-made wreaths, garlands, and topiaries, and supplies.

The Homested
Waynesberg, PA
(412) 852 2338
Dried flowers, ready-made wreaths, garlands, and topiaries.

Leaman's Applebarn
Freeland, MI
(517) 695 2465
Dried flowers, ready-made wreaths, garlands, and topiaries, and some floral-arts supplies.

Lee Wards
1200 South Charles Street
Elgin, IL. 60120
(708) 888 5800

Lexington Gardens
1008 Lexington Avenue
New York, NY 10021
(212) 861 4390
Ready-made wreaths, garlands, and topiaries; accepts custom orders.

Lewiscraft 40
Commander Boulevard
Scarborough, Ontario Mls 3S2 Canada
(416) 291 8406
Dried flowers, and supplies ; mail-order service available.

Lewis Mountain Herbs and Everlastings
2345 State Route 247
Manchester, OH 45144
(513) 549 2484
Dried flowers, ready-made wreaths, garlands, and topiaries, and floral-arts supplies; mail-order service available.

Manhattan Fruitier
210 East Sixth Street
New York, NY 10003
(212) 260 2280
Culinary wreaths.

Mid-Island Floral Supply
602 Pineaire Drive
Bay Shore, NY
(516) 586 6111
Dried flowers and floral-arts supplies.

Naturally Yours
Santa Maria, CA
(805) 922 6184
Freeze-dried flowers, ready-made wreaths,
garlands, and topiaries, and floral-arts supplies.

Preserve the Memories
Cheshire, CT
(203) 620 0477
Freeze-dried flowers and ready-made wreaths,
garlands, and topiaries.

Rathdowney Ltd.
3 River Street
Bethel, VT 05032
(802) 234 9928
Dried flowers, ready-made wreaths, garlands,
and topiaries, floral-arts supplies; mail-order
service available.

Smith & Hawken
25 Corte Madera
Mill Valley, CA 94941
(415) 381 1800
Topiaries; mail-order available.

Sura Kayla
484 Broome Street
New York, NY 10013
(212) 941 8757
Dried flowers, ready-made wreaths, garlands,
and topiaries; floral-arts supplies can be special ordered; mailing list.

Twigs
1305 Madison Avenue
New York, NY
(212) 369 4000
Ready-made wreaths, garlands, and topiaries;
accepts custom orders.

Village Flowers
297 Main Street
Huntington, NY 11743
(516) 427 0996
Ready-made wreaths, garlands, and topiaries;
custom orders accepted.

VSF
204 West 10th Street
New York, NY 10014
(212) 206 7236
Dried flowers, ready-made seasonal wreaths,
garlands, and topiaries, and floral-arts supplies.

Zeze
398 East 52nd Street
New York, NY 10022
(212) 753 7767
Seasonal wreaths, garlands, and topiaries, and
floral-arts supplies; occasionally carries dried
flowers.

RIBBON

Vaban Ribbons International
2070 C Boston Drive
Atlanta, GA 30337
(800) 822 2606

MAIL-ORDER CATALOGS

The following list of catalogs allows you the
convenience of ordering your materials
and/or finished arrangements by mail. Some
companies specialize in wreaths and garlands
for the holidays only.

Bay Laurel Farm
West Garzaz Road
Carmel Valley, CA 93924
(408) 059 2913

Calyx & Corolla
1550 Bryant Street #900
San Francisco, CA 94103
(800) 877 7836

Crate and Barrel
P.O. Box 9059
Wheeling, IL. 60090
(800) 323 5461

Eddie Bauer
P.O. Box 3700
Seattle, WA 98124
(800) 426 8020

Fox Hill Farm
143 West Michigan Avenue
P.O. Box 9
Parma, MI 49269
(517) 531 3179

Gardener's Eden
P.O. Box 7307
San Francisco, CA 94120-7307
(800) 822 9600

The Herb Farm
Barnard Road
Granville, MA 01034
(413) 357 8882

Lindemann AG Company
2817 West Locust Avenue
Fresno, CA 93711
(209) 449 1230

Petals
1 Acqueduct Road
White Plains, NY 10606
(800) 431-2464

Sassafras Herbs Shop
636 Farrell Parkway
P.O. Box 50192
Nashville, TN 37203
(615) 832 2962

Smith & Hawken
25 Corte Madera
Mill Valley, CA 94941
(415) 383-2000

Williams-Sonoma
P.O. Box 7456
San Francisco, CA 94120
(800) 541 2233

ASSOCIATIONS

The American Association for the Dried and
Preserved Floral Industry
(AAD and PFI)
P.O. Box 171
Lenox Hill Station, NY 10021
(800) 359 7601

SUGGESTED READING

❧ Black, Penny. *A Passion for Flowers*. New York: Simon & Schuster, 1992.

❧ Condor, Susan. *Dried Flowers*. Boston: David R. Godine, 1988.

❧ Hillier, Malcolm and Colin Hilton. *The Book of Dried Flowers*. New York: Simon & Schuster, 1986.

❧ Ohrbach, Barbara Milo. *The Scented Room*. New York: Clarkson Potter, Inc., 1986.

❧ Petelin, Carol. *The Creative Guide to Dried Flowers*. London: Webb & Bower, Inc., 1988.

❧ Pulleyn, Rob. *The Wreath Book*. New York: Sterling Publishing Co., 1990.

❧ Sheen, Joanna and Caroline Alexander. *Dried Flower Gardening*. London: Ward Lock, 1991.

❧ Tolley, Emelie and Chris Mead. *Gifts from the Herb Garden*. New York: Clarkson Potter, 1991.

❧ Turner, Kenneth. Flower Style: *The Art of Floral Design and Decoration*. New York: Weidenfeld & Nicolson, 1989.